DATE DUE

NOV 2 8 2005	JAN 2 4 2006	

DEMCO 38-296

EYE OPENERS

Holidays

BLACKBIRCH®
PRESS

THOMSON
GALE

San Diego • Detroit • New York • San Francisco • Cleveland
New Haven, Conn. • Waterville, Maine • London • Munich

For more information, contact
The Gale Group, Inc.
27500 Drake Rd.
Farmington Hills, MI 48331-3535
Or you can visit our Internet site at http://www.gale.com

LIBRARY OF CONGRESS CATALOGING-IN-PUBLICATION DATA

Nathan, Emma.
  Holidays / by Emma Nathan.
    p. cm. — (Eyeopeners series)
  Includes index.
  Summary: Discusses celebrations from countries around the world for such holidays as
Carnaval, Passover, Winterlude, Cinco de Mayo, and Easter.
  ISBN 1-56711-650-7 (hardback : alk. paper)
  1. Holidays—Juvenile literature. [1. Holidays.] I. Title. II. Series: Nathan, Emma.
Eyeopeners series.

GT3933 .N36 2003
394.26—dc21

2002014083

Printed in United States
10 9 8 7 6 5 4 3 2 1

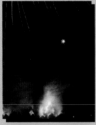

TABLE OF CONTENTS

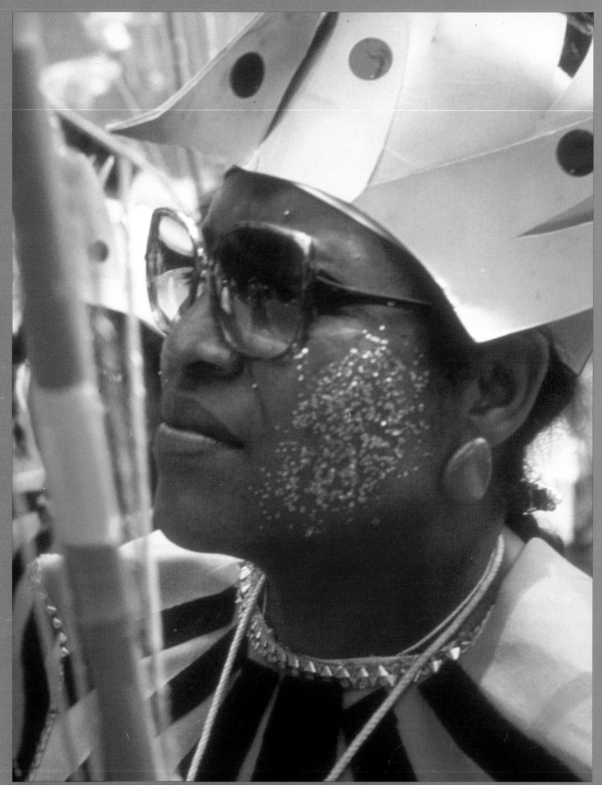

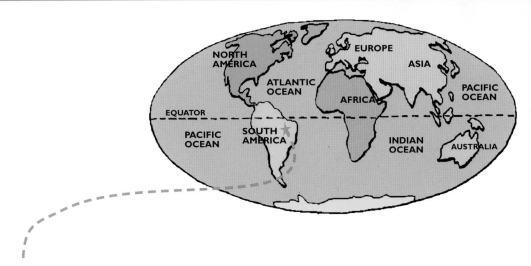

BRAZIL (bra-ZILL)

Brazil is on the continent of South America. It is the largest country in South America.

People in Brazil hold a special celebration 40 days before Easter.

The celebration is called Carnaval.

During Carnaval, people dress up in fancy costumes. They dance and have parades.

◀ **Woman dressed for Carnaval**

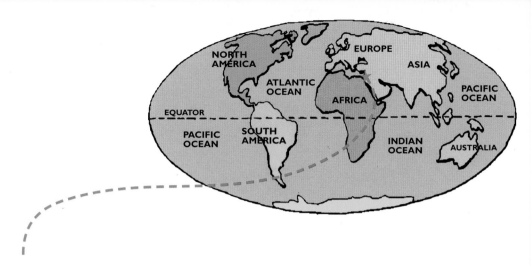

ISRAEL (IZ-rayl)

Israel is on the continent of Asia. It is in a part of Asia called the Middle East.

Many people in Israel are Jews.

Passover is an important Jewish holiday in Israel.

During Passover a big special meal is made. It is called a seder (SAY-der).

During the seder stories from the Old Testament are told. Special foods in the seder are part of the stories.

◀ **Passover seder in Israel**

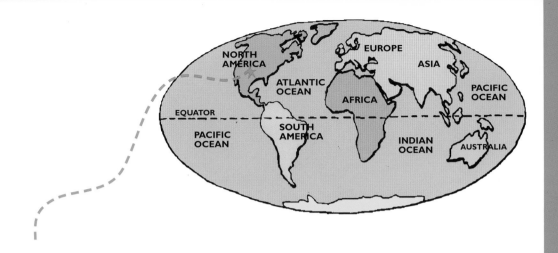

UNITED STATES (yu-nye-ted STAYTS)

The United States is on the continent of North America.

More than 200 years ago, America was ruled by England.

On July 4, 1776, the Declaration of Independence said America would no longer be ruled by England.

Americans celebrate July 4 every year. Fireworks and barbecues are very popular ways to celebrate.

◀ **Fourth of July fireworks**

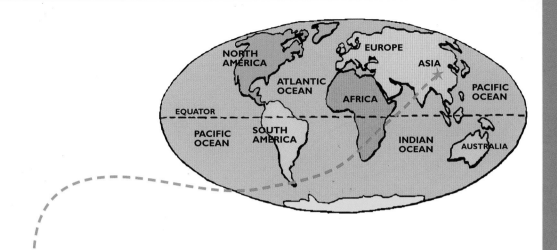

CHINA (CHY-nuh)

China is on the continent of Asia.

Chinese New Year is a very important holiday in China. People celebrate for many days.

Parades, fireworks, and colorful costumes are all a part of the holiday.

Families give each other gifts wrapped in red paper. Red is the color of luck in China.

◀ Giant dragon display for Chinese New Year

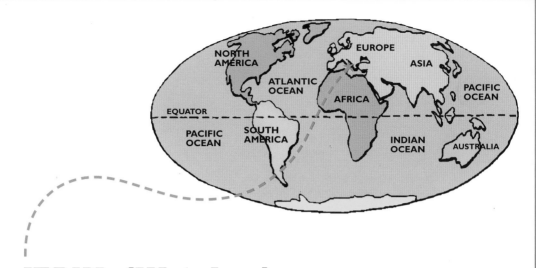

ITALY (IH-tul-ee)

Italy is on the continent of Europe.

People in the city of Venice hold a celebration every February.

The celebration is a pre-Lent festival. It happens about 40 days before Easter.

The festival is famous for its fancy masks and colorful costumes.

◀ **People at Venice festival**

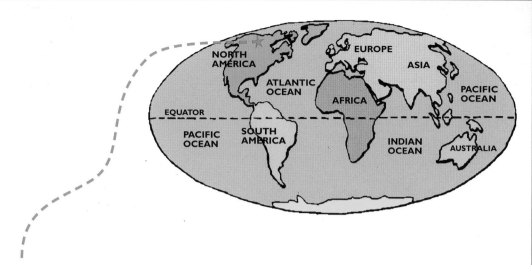

CANADA (CAN-a-duh)

Canada is on the continent of North America.

Every January, people in the city of Ottowa celebrate Winterlude.

Winterlude is a time to enjoy winter fun.

During Winterlude, people skate on the world's largest ice rink.

Local artists and teams from other countries create huge sculptures from ice and snow.

◀ **Winterlude festival in Ottawa**

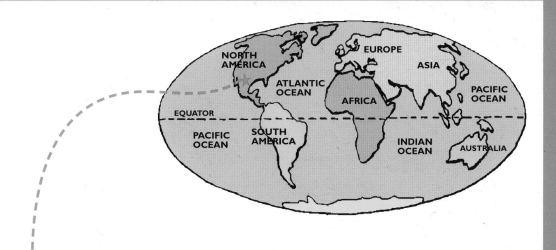

MEXICO (MEKKS-ih-ko)

Mexico is on the continent of North America.

Cinco de Mayo (sin-ko deh my-o) is a holiday that celebrates independence.

Cinco de Mayo means May 5th in Spanish. On May 5th, 1862, Mexico beat the French army.

Parades and outdoor festivals are popular ways to celebrate.

Many Mexican Americans celebrate Cinco de Mayo.

◀ Cinco de Mayo parade

17

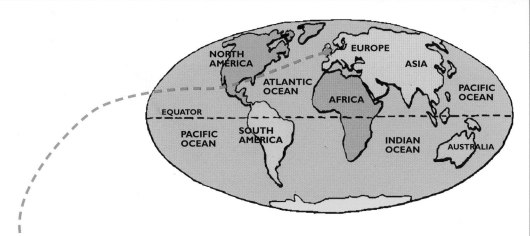

Map showing: NORTH AMERICA, EUROPE, ASIA, ATLANTIC OCEAN, AFRICA, PACIFIC OCEAN, EQUATOR, PACIFIC OCEAN, SOUTH AMERICA, INDIAN OCEAN, AUSTRALIA

UNITED KINGDOM
(yu-nye-ted KING-dum)

The United Kingdom is part of Europe.

In the United Kingdom, November 5 is
Guy Fawkes Day.

Guy Fawkes is a villain from England's history.

People celebrate Guy Fawkes Day with giant
fires and fireworks.

Some people dress up in costume and burn dolls
that are supposed to represent Guy Fawkes.

◀ **Bonfire and fireworks on Guy Fawkes Day**

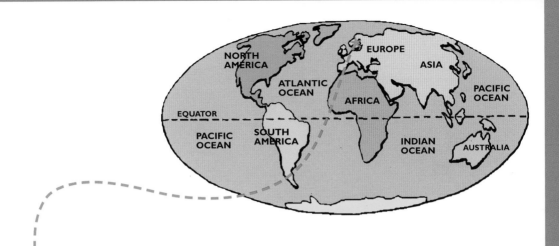

SWEDEN (SWEE-den)

Sweden is on the continent of Europe.

Every summer, people in Sweden celebrate the longest day of the year.

On this day in Sweden, the sun never sets.

The celebration is called Midsummer Festival.

During Midsummer Festival, children pick flowers and decorate poles.

Children then dance around the decorated poles.

◀ **Midsummer Festival**

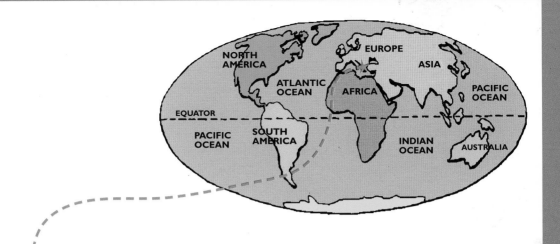

GREECE (greese)

Greece is part of the continent of Europe.

In Greece, Easter comes in late March or early April.

On the Saturday before Greek Easter, families celebrate by eating eggs dyed red.

On Easter Sunday, families toss red eggs. The person with the last egg that is not cracked is supposed to have good luck.

◀ **Greek dancing for celebration**

Index

For More Information

Websites

History of Holidays
http://www.billpetro.com/HolidayHistory/default.htm

Holidays Around the World
http://falcon.jmu.edu/~ramseyil/holidays.htm

Books

Angell, Carole S. *Celebrations Around the World.* Fulcrum Publishing, 1996.

Jones, Lynda. *Kids Around the World Celebrate! The Best Feasts and Festivals from Many Lands.* New York: John Wiley, 1999.

Markham, Lois. *World Celebrations and Ceremonies: Harvest.* San Diego: Blackbirch Press/Gale, 1998

Spirn, Michelle. *World Celebrations and Ceremonies: New Year.* San Diego: Blackbirch Press/Gale, 1998